PARTIES

FOR KIDS

Contributing Writers

Michaeline Bresnahan

Joan Macfarlane

Publications International, Ltd.

Louis Weber, C.E.O.
Publications International, Ltd.
7373 North Cicero Avenue
Lincolnwood, Illinois 60646

ISBN 0-7853-0533-5

Michaeline Bresnahan and **Joan Macfarlane** are co-authors of *The Happiest Birthdays* and *The No-Sew Costume Book.* Together they operate a custom-designed children's party business. Michaeline is also a free-lance crafts consultant. Joan is a former associate editor with *Good Housekeeping* magazine.

Photography on pages 36 and 50 by Sanders Studios, Inc.
Food Stylist: Mary Helen Steindler

Photography and food styling on cover (UL) and on pages 14, 30, 46, and 56 by Burke/Triolo Studio.

Photography on page 61 (LR) by Siede/Preis Photography.

Remaining photography by Sacco Productions Limited/Chicago
Photographers: Chris Brooks, Peter Ross
Photo Stylist: Melissa J. Sacco
Production: Roberta Ellis, Paula Walters
Royal Model Management models: Nicholas Babladelis, Mary Beth Johnson, Roderick Jordan, Eddie Mahra, Ann Svane, Tabitha Vasquez.

Diagrams on pages 14, 31, 37, 47, and 57 drawn by Rowena J. Vargas.

Contac® is a registered trademark of Rubbermaid Incorporated.

Velcro® is a registered trademark of Velcro USA.

CONTENTS

INTRODUCTION • 4

CLOWNING AROUND • 10

SUPERHEROES • 16

MERMAID MADNESS • 18

DIGGING DINOS • 24

FAST TRACK • 32

FASHION DOLL PARTY • 38

ROYAL BALL • 42

FRIGHT NIGHT • 48

CREATURES FROM OUTER SPACE • 52

CAROLING PARTY • 58

PARTY SHORTS • 62

INTRODUCTION

Kids love parties! They look forward to them with great anticipation. They not only want to have fun, they expect to have fun! Parents, on the other hand, aren't always as enthusiastic, especially when it's their turn to host the gathering! Throwing a party for kids can seem like an awesome responsibility. It often ruffles the feathers of even the most secure parents. But it doesn't have to. With the right attitude and some planning and preparation, memorable parties can be another one of your specialties!

Choose a Theme

Choosing a party theme is like choosing a Halloween costume. Some children (and parents) work best if a few choices are given; others know what they want before they even know if it's available! When choosing a party theme, work with your child in the manner he or she is most comfortable—giving a few choices or asking the child straight out what kind of party he/she wants. Often a party can be built around a single activity that really appeals to your child. Flip through this book on your own or with your child for inspiration. There are many different possibilities to choose from. Use any of the parties as described, modify one or more to your needs, or simply use the ideas as inspiration for creating your own personalized party! However you do it, try to reflect your party theme in the invitations, games, decorations, and favors. Repeating or elaborating on a single theme seems to please children most and makes planning the party easier.

Select an Invitation

The invitation is your first contact with the guests. It gives you an opportunity to engage them, create anticipation, and to entertain them, too! You may be lucky enough to find the perfect invitation by hunting through the racks of traditional store-bought cards, but more often than not, creating your own invitations is a more attention-getting and fun solution. Each party in this book includes an easy-to-make, out-of-the-ordinary invitation with instructions. These invitations are designed to lend themselves to variations and personalizing, so let your creative juices flow and have fun with them!

Fill in the Details

While filling out and mailing invitations two weeks in advance seems like a very small piece of the party puzzle, it involves making several decisions that can affect the success of your party. Deciding on the number of children to be invited and the length of the party are two of the most critical decisions you will make. The general rule on numbers is the age of your child plus one.

There are no rules on party length, but the most common mistake is to make the party too long. It is not necessary to have custody of the children before they can have a good time! One to one and one-half hours is generally sufficient for preschoolers; two to two and one-half hours suits the elementary-school set just fine. Sleep-overs are a special case. Planning to have children arrive at dinner or dessert time and leave after breakfast—with clearly set arrival and departure times—is a "minimum" sleep-over.

Aside from the standard party details of name, time, place, and R.S.V.P., any special requests of the guests or their parents should also be included on the invitation. Special requests might include asking parents of two- or three-year-old children to be prepared (if not required) to remain during the party, dress requirements (e.g., jeans, casual dress, outdoor clothing, bathing suits, costumes, etc.), items to be brought along for game or activity requirements (e.g., flashlights, makeup), rain dates, and inflexible arrival times (e.g., when an outing is planned) to name some of the possibilities.

Plan and Prepare

The absolute first thing you should do in advance of the party is to get a commitment from at least one other adult to help on the day of the party. A baby-sitter or friend will fill the bill, saving you from panic and exhaustion come party day!

After this requirement is fulfilled, your next best move is to create a party schedule. Planning the sequence of the party games and activities, the projects, and food in advance will make the whole party process run smoother, both before and during the event. When figuring out the beginning of your party strategy, keep in mind that guests arrive gradually. Choose a party opener that guests can drop in on as they arrive without disruption, such as adding artwork to a paper roll birthday banner. Also consider the space or location you will be working with and how the party will flow—some games and projects tie up a room or space for the entire length of the party or from the beginning until completion.

The second group of preparations involves getting all the necessary components for games and craft projects ready before the party. It's definitely a good idea to try out the craft projects yourself ahead of time, not only to have a sample finished product on hand, but to give you better knowledge of the materials and the assistance the kids may need come party time. Pay attention to the details and prepare for the unexpected. A good rule of thumb when preparing for any craft project or when making hats or other decorative garb for the guests is to always have the makings for one or two more guests than expected.

A final note on this point is to set yourself up so you're organized at party time. Patience is not likely to be the guests' long suit, given all the excitement. Passing out the materials and giving instructions should be done as quickly and easily as possible!

Choosing Party Games

Planning and preparing for specific party games should begin with the selection of age-appropriate activities. This has been done in the parties included in this book. Age-appropriate, in the case of younger children, not only means that the games should not require physical or mental skills they don't have, it also means that the games be somehow non-competitive. Everyone should get a "prize." As children grow older, competitive games at parties are more tolerable and eventually more desirable. In every case, hospitality requires the acknowledgment of all guests on some level.

The tokens or prizes for each game could be one of the party props, such as the dinosaur headdress, or they could be small purchased mementos. At all parties, the games and activities should include a balanced selection of active, quiet, physical, and mental challenges to keep the party energy high, without being explosive. To safeguard against extra, unfilled activity time, always be prepared with a stash of traditional games, such as clothespins in the bottle; musical chairs; Who Am I?; Duck, Duck, Goose; etc.

Feeding the Crowd

Food planning and preparations can present an opportunity for real creativity; however, always keep the audience in mind! Children are generally not adventurous eaters, and they are usually not very interested in food at parties, except when it comes to sweets! Why fight it? Make dessert the feasting focal point—and do it in style! Many child-appealing possibilities are featured in this book. The "shape" cakes, such as the clown and dinosaur, require only minimal skill to achieve a dramatic look. For best results, lightly freeze the cake you'll be working with. Draw your desired picture on a piece of paper, using as much of the paper for the design as possible; cut this pattern out along the outline. Lay the pattern directly on top of the cake and cut along the pattern edge with a sharp knife held perpendicular to the cake. Carefully brush away any crumbs, then frost the entire cake. Use candies, sprinkles, and other delicious tidbits like fruit slices, peanuts, pretzels, etc., to create the drawing on the cake and add texture. Try densely packed sprinkles, chocolate chips, or peanut butter chips to simulate flat fur; thin pretzel sticks or clipped shoestring licorice stuck straight into the cake for three-dimensional fur; giant gum balls or marshmallows with a black jelly bean in the center for eyes; fruit slices for scales; candy corn, white candy-coated gum, or mini-marshmallows for teeth; and densely sprinkled, clipped red shoestring licorice for lips. When adding the candies, try to make the flavors as compatible as possible—chocolate cakes with chocolate and mint-based candies, peanuts and pretzels, or cookies and lemon cakes with fruit-flavored and sour candies.

When serving a main meal, we generally recommend sticking with the old standbys—hamburgers, hot dogs, pizza, and peanut butter and jelly sandwiches. If you really have the urge to get creative, give the regulars an upbeat name, like dinoburgers; cut simple sandwiches into fun shapes with the aid of cookie cutters; or stack fresh fruit and marshmallows on fancy toothpicks.

Setting the Scene

The idea of decorations usually conjures up visions of streamers and balloons, the standard fare of many parties. In this book, we have presented festive hats and garb, "big-effect" game props, and great-looking projects and favors that all work together to create a dramatic visual effect. Investing your money this way is more cost effective—these decorations are not simply paper throwaways! In the cases where we have suggested room decorations, such as posters, maps, hanging fish, or store signs, they are used to create a specific location—an underwater world or a western town, for example.

Creating a party atmosphere outdoors requires different considerations. Somehow, a bunch of kids running around in the backyard seems more like an everyday occurrence than having them all indoors for the party. Decorating trees, swing sets, fences, and shrubs really heightens the party atmosphere. Corrugated cutouts of animals can peek through the bushes, cutout fish can be hung from limbs of trees, simple signs can be hung around to give the feel of a town, a tree can

be decorated for home base, and streamers can be twisted around a swing set.

Selecting Special Entertainment

A successful party does not require an adult dressed like a superhero or clown. With younger age groups, less is often more, and parties at home are still the most fun. When entertainment or outings are planned, make sure they are age-appropriate and fresh. Put your money elsewhere if the only options are repeats of other friends' birthday parties. If the entertainment choice serves as a passive activity, such as a puppet show or story-telling, have some physical activities to round out the party. When an outing is planned or the entire party will be held at a public place, such as a bowling alley, ball field, or the theater, personalize the event with fabulous party favors, creative foods, or simple, theme-oriented games. The Party Shorts chapter includes suggestions for athletic events.

Favors

We have suggested game and activity prizes that are really party favors collected throughout the party. Some are handmade, some are purchased, and some are made by the children at the party. As with all other aspects, thematic consistency is desirable. When shopping for favors, keep your eyes open in all kinds of stores. Often the best finds are being sold as something other than "toys" (e.g., shell soaps!). Nature stores, museum shops, catalogs, etc., can all be searched for the right favors. One tip to remember is that sets of stamps, animals, stickers, etc., can often be broken up. This represents a savings in money and often allows a wider range of choice.

Enjoying the Party

Armed with a plan, setup, and prepared with extra games in your hip pocket, nothing can really go wrong. It is even possible to relax and enjoy the children as you move through the party with them. Before you know it, the party is over and has become a fabulous memory.

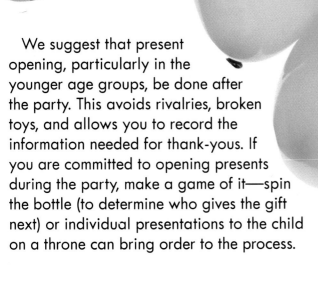

We suggest that present opening, particularly in the younger age groups, be done after the party. This avoids rivalries, broken toys, and allows you to record the information needed for thank-yous. If you are committed to opening presents during the party, make a game of it—spin the bottle (to determine who gives the gift next) or individual presentations to the child on a throne can bring order to the process.

Extending Thanks

While thank-you notes are not an absolute must, they are a considerate way to communicate your and your child's gratitude. A thank-you note can be as simple as photocopied messages and artwork, computer-generated prints and art, or as complex as handwritten note cards and thank-you cards. Address the note to the guest (rather than the parent) and have your child sign the notes when possible.

Have Fun

Having fun is what this is all about. Share the good times with your child. Good memories are precious commodities and caring goes a long way! Party on!

CLOWNING AROUND

The easy, free spirit of this clown theme party will be pure fun for the littlest party-goers.

Invitation

A dimensional CLOWN FACE MAGNET invitation delivers the party message and then sticks around on the refrigerator as a reminder of good times ahead. Draw or trace a simple clown face and collar. Make a template

PUT ON A HAPPY FACE!

IT'S BIRTHDAY PARTY TIME FOR JAMES!

WHEN: JULY 11TH
TIME: NOON TO 3:00
WHERE: 123 OAK AVENUE
RSVP: 555-1515

from the outline. Using heavy drawing paper, cut out a clown face for each invitation. Add the details—hat, eyes, mouth, etc.—using marking pens, glitter (or glitter pens), and markers. Use a piece of lace, plain or gathered, or eyelet trim for the collar; glue it in place. On the back of the card, write the party information with a ballpoint pen (you don't want the ink to bleed through), leaving space to attach a small piece of magnetic tape (available at craft and hardware stores). Hand-stamping may be necessary for more dimensional clowns!

Hats~Decorations

In the spirit of the big top, kids will be turned into fancy clowns. CLOWN COLLARS PLUS can be made by cutting a 28 × 11-inch rectangle from brightly colored felt, and a 12-inch diameter circle from white felt. Trim to round the corners of the rectangle. Scallop the edges of the circle. Lay the circle with the edge beginning 5 inches from one end of the rectangle. Secure with glue. Fold the assembled piece along the center of the white scalloped collar. Cut a 6-inch diameter scoop along the fold line for the neck hole. Add a short slit at the back of the circle so the collar fits over the child's head. Decorate the front with pompons, felt dots, or flowers. Make one for each guest.

when they realize they will be part of a circus parade. A large, abstract shape cut from poster board is prepared for each child in advance. The shapes do not need to be identical, but they should be roughly the same size. Funny bits and pieces of colored paper, felt, and wads of tissue paper are then attached by the children using large dot stickers and glue sticks. Pieces of yarn, rick-rack, and pipe cleaners can be laced through holes at the edges of the shape. Smaller dot stickers can be stuck on, too! Finish the parade stick for the kids by stapling it to a paper tube (covered in Contac paper, tissue paper, or spray-painted), like those found inside wrapping paper.

To top off the costume, make a painter's hat CLOWN HAT (see photo on page 10). Thick yarn or large chenille on light wire can be used to add hair. Without cutting, tie or wind a clump of the chosen trim into a dumbbell shape with the center long enough to cross the head. Position the hair on your child before attaching it. Tack the hair-piece at the top and sides of the inside of the cap slightly toward the back. Turn the cap around when wearing it.

Choose brightly colored decorations to create a striped big-top mood. The project and game pieces will finish the look.

Project

Very young children will enjoy decorating colorful, crazy look-ing PARADE STICKS, especially

Activities~Games

CLOWN TOSS is a challenge that even the youngest clowns can meet! A large, colorful poster-board clown (backed with corrugated cardboard) with a wide-open mouth becomes a good target for little hands to shoot wads of tissue paper through. Hanging the clown in a doorway protects it during the game. Occasionally, the adult on the other side can blow bubbles through the clown's mouth, or throw wrapped popcorn balls out for the children to chase and catch. A horn honking or bell ringing when the kids are successful will delight everyone, even those who mostly miss the target. Prizes should be given to all the kids when a certain number of tissue wads fly through.

PARTY BAGS, made from brown paper shopping bags with added yarn handles, can be decorated with stickers while the children wait for all the guests to arrive.

CLOWN FACES can be added to those children willing to be made up. A red nose and a small design on the cheeks—hearts, stars, butterflies, stripes—will complete the look. Beyond your basic face-paint or makeup,

tatoos and/or stickers are a plus. Remember, not all clowns will want to have makeup applied!

After being dressed up and made up, a CLOWN PARADE is a natural. Carrying their PARADE STICKS, the children march "follow-the-leader" style, snaking and shaking to the best of circus music.

CLOWNING AROUND

Cake~Food

CLOWN CAKE

CAKES & FROSTINGS
- 1 (9-inch) square cake
- 1 (9-inch) round cake
- 1½ cups Base Frosting (see page 15), if desired
- 3 cups Buttercream Frosting (see page 15)*

DECORATIONS & EQUIPMENT
- Assorted candies
- 1 (19×13-inch) cake board, cut to fit cake, if desired, and covered
- Pastry bags, medium writing tip, and star tip

1. Trim tops and edges of cakes. Cut square cake as shown in diagram 1.

2. Position pieces on prepared cake board as shown in diagram 2, connecting with some of the white frosting.

3. Frost entire cake with Base Frosting to seal in crumbs.

4. Frost face with white frosting. Using writing tip and pink frosting, pipe mouth.

5. Frost bow tie and top of hat with yellow frosting as shown in photo. Frost hat with some of the orange frosting. Using star tip and orange frosting, pipe design on hat and bow tie.

6. Arrange assorted candies as shown.

Makes 16 to 18 servings

Color ¾ cup frosting orange, ½ cup yellow, and ¼ cup pink; reserve 1½ cups white frosting.

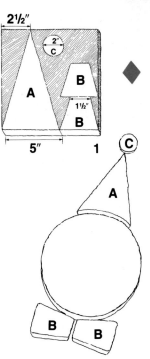

With the big-top music still playing, slide into CLOWN FREEZE. Children dance around and act silly to the music. When the music stops they must freeze in place.

The PEANUT HUNT, an old standby, is actually thrilling to small children and quite appropriate given the theme.

14

BASE FROSTING
3 cups powdered sugar, sifted
½ cup butter or margarine, softened
¼ cup milk
½ teaspoon vanilla

Combine powdered sugar, butter, milk, and vanilla in large bowl. Beat with electric mixer until smooth. Add more milk, 1 teaspoon at a time. Frosting should be fairly thin.

Makes about 2 cups

BUTTERCREAM FROSTING
6 cups powdered sugar, sifted and divided
¾ cup butter or margarine, softened
¼ cup shortening
6 to 8 tablespoons milk, divided
1 teaspoon vanilla

Combine 3 cups powdered sugar, butter, shortening, 4 tablespoons milk, and vanilla in large bowl. Beat with electric mixer until smooth. Add remaining powdered sugar; beat until light and fluffy, adding more milk, 1 tablespoon at a time, as needed for good spreading consistency.

Makes about 3½ cups

CLOWN ICE CREAM CONES are made by placing a scoop of ice cream on a plate and topping it with an ice cream cone hat. Press in two raisins and bits of cherries for the eyes and mouth. Whipped cream from a pressurized container delivers the perfect collar and hat pompon for this character.

Entertainment

There are many children's videos on the clown theme, as well as live entertainment (clowns, jugglers, acrobats, balloon artists). A circus story, read aloud, is a home-grown way to elaborate on the theme. Limit any entertainment to between 20 and 30 minutes. Also remember that some young children are easily frightened by the sight of people in costumes, like clowns.

Favors

The clown collar and hat make great party favors. And the kids will want to hang onto their parade sticks. Other great favors include juggling bean bags, rubber balls, foam clown noses and clown makeup, horns to honk, whistles, inflatable circus animals, funny socks or gloves, giant ties, circus stickers, coloring books, or storybooks.

SUPERHEROES

Playing on children's adoration of superheroes, this party puts the partygoers in the spotlight, making them the stars of the day!

Invitation

Creating your own SUPERHERO CARTOON STRIP or framing one of your favorites from the funny pages is the perfect ticket to a super event. If you choose to make your own cartoon, remember to keep it simple. Use legal-size paper, so the invitation fits into a standard enve-lope, and fold it into equal thirds; trim away one section, leaving a folded card. Draw the cartoon on the front section. Include the party details under the cartoon (as in the photo) or on the inside.

Hats~Decorations

To make each SUPERHERO CAPE, simply cut a ¾-yard rectangle of 45-inch (or more)-wide black, nonravel fabric. Fold over 1½ inches along one edge to the inside and sew or glue (using a thin line) close to the cut edge to form a casing. Thread a long piece of 1-inch-wide ribbon through the casing, leaving enough ribbon at both edges to tie a bow. Tack or glue the ribbon in place at the casing edges.

To make the POWER PATCHES, draw a series of 3-inch circles on paper. Draw a "power" symbol inside each—an owl for wisdom, a muscular arm for strength, a shoe with wings for running, a ghost for invisibility, a cat for multiple lives, an eye for X-ray vision, an ear for supersonic hearing, and a frog for leaping ability—using simple line drawings that fit within the circles; cut out the symbol patterns. Cut the symbols and 3-inch circles from different felt colors. Glue a power symbol on each circle. Make multiples of the patches, so there are plenty to go around! To secure the patches to the capes, use Velcro fasteners or safety pins.

Project

SUPERHERO INSIGNIA—Starting with an 8-inch circular felt base, fabric pens and paints, feathers, sequins, felt scraps, yarns, glue, and other interesting notions, the children create their own hero insignias. Make a sample or two to stimulate their

imaginations. When complete, the insignias can be pinned onto the cape.

Activities~Games

POWER PLAY—Participating in a series of physical and mental challenges, the children test their powers and are awarded power patches for succeeding. Following are possible challenges (that can be done individually or in relays) and their respective patches: running race (winged shoe), camouflaged object scavenger hunt (ghost), and superhero trivia (owl). Not everyone has to win every patch, but be sure that the kids all get their fair share!

Cake~Food

To renew the heroes' strength after the challenges, consider serving brownie-and-ice cream POWER BARS with whipped cream and a cherry for a super sundae!

Favors

Consider superhero comic books, figurines, posters, face masks, or other memorabilia.

MERMAID MADNESS

A kid-cultural obsession with mermaids makes this a favorite party theme. Blended with aquatic illusion and underwater friends, it is likely that "mermaid mania" will be catching!

Invitation

Calling all mermaids! The STARFISH NECKLACE INVITATION, a simple folded card shaped like a starfish, will get the party off to a swimming start. To make the starfish, draw the shape on folded heavy paper with one edge along the fold, and cut it out. Decorate and pierce two holes in the top starfish. Lace an 18-inch piece of yarn through and tie the ends in a bow. If you wish, draw a dot-

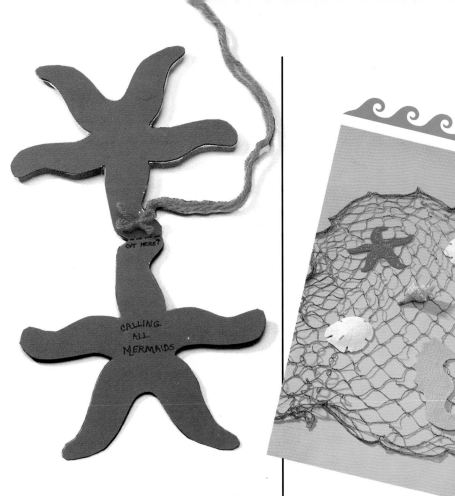

ted line and write "Cut Here" on the fold inside. The invitation then separates into a necklace for young mermaids and a party reminder for Mom!

Hats~Decorations

A CORAL CROWN cut free-hand from stiff poster board is the perfect adornment for little mermaids. Adding a starfish with double-stick tape to the center of the crown and glitter details give the crown depth and shimmer.

Create the illusion of being underwater with water-colored blue and green streamers and strips of netting, and aqua friends—fish, starfish, and jelly-fish—hung from the ceiling.

Make the doorway an entry into an underwater world, using lots of streamers and net strips for mermaids to "swim" through.

Project

Rehabilitate the octopus's reputation by making friendly creatures that just love to wear sea jewelry. The FRIENDLY OCTOPUS to be decorated by the children is simply made from poster board and a balloon of the same color. The finished leg piece will be roughly 20 inches in diameter. Drawing a 4-inch circle on the center of the poster board and

lines that divide the circle into eight equal segments will guide you in creating the perfect leg piece. Draw legs—one radiating from each line in the circle—that roughly fill the poster board. When cutting out the leg piece

do not cut into the circle. Put a small slit in the center of the circle for the knot on the inflated balloon to be pulled through. Eyes can be made from tape, Contac paper, or plain white mailing labels. A $2\frac{1}{2} \times 1\frac{1}{2}$-inch-wide oval, with a small rectangle

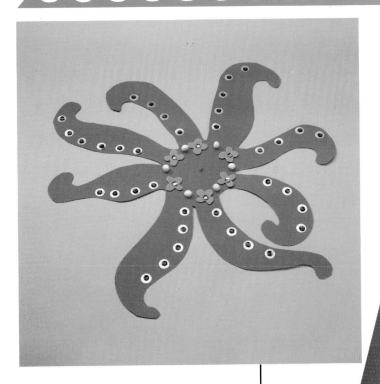

of colored label or black Contac paper added slightly above center, makes a great octopus eye. Make a leg piece, a pair of eyes, and a blown-up balloon for each child before the party.

The children will be adding decorations to the octopus leg pieces. Some items for decorating are paper-hole reinforcers, colored pasta, aluminum foil and pipe cleaner rings, strung and loose sequins, felt flowers, pompons, and tiny tissue paper wads. If the children decorate their octopus at the beginning of the party, white glue will have time to dry before they go home.

Have extra balloons on hand in case any pop.

Activities~Games

SEA SEARCHING for underwater treasures—"pearl" popbeads, gold coins, starfish necklaces (above), candy fish wrapped in plastic wrap, little seashells—generates more than the usual amount of enthusiasm when the children are given decorated "treasure chests" to store their loot in.

FISH SCHOOL is an elaborate game in which black and more

MERMAID MADNESS

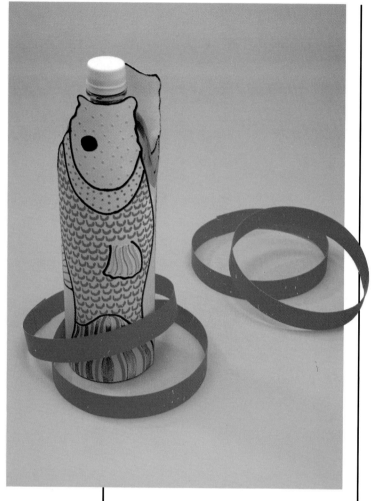

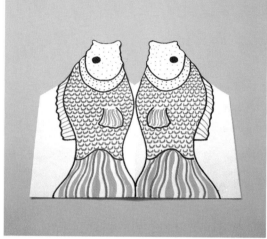

SWIMMING CONTESTS, in which teams of children perform imaginary swimming strokes (the crab stroke, the flounder stroke, the mermaid stroke, the sea horse stroke), are a pretty funny way to race through air.

FISH RING TOSS is an exciting ring toss game made by covering plastic soda bottles with fish sleeves. The sleeves are made by taping the open ends of a piece of paper on which two vertical fish are drawn to cover the soda bottles. The rings, made from thin strips of poster board taped together, can be of different sizes. The more fish and rings the merrier!

mermaidish-colored balloons filling a room are "tamed." Children are directed to separate the black "sharks" from the other fish in a short amount of time without actually holding the balloons—blowing, shuffling with feet, or patting with hands according to your directions. Store the balloons in garbage bags until the game begins.

DANCING MERMAIDS will possibly be everyone's favorite activity at the party. Interpretive dancing to mermaid music is jazzed up with the addition of scarves made from fabric netting. If and when the children get too wild, a game of music freeze (stop the music to make mermaid statues!) gets things back under control.

Cake~Food

When the children swim to the table they will be greeted by a FLOUNDER CAKE. A 9 × 13-inch cake, cut in a simple chubby fish shape, is easily transformed into a flounder using yellow frosting and blue gel.

Favors

Children will be returning with their crowns, sea treasure and treasure chest, and decorated octopus. They would also love real seashells, shell soaps or papers, figurines, penny whistles, mermaid stencils, water toys, etc. Nature stores, seasonal stores, and shell collector outlets may vary your options.

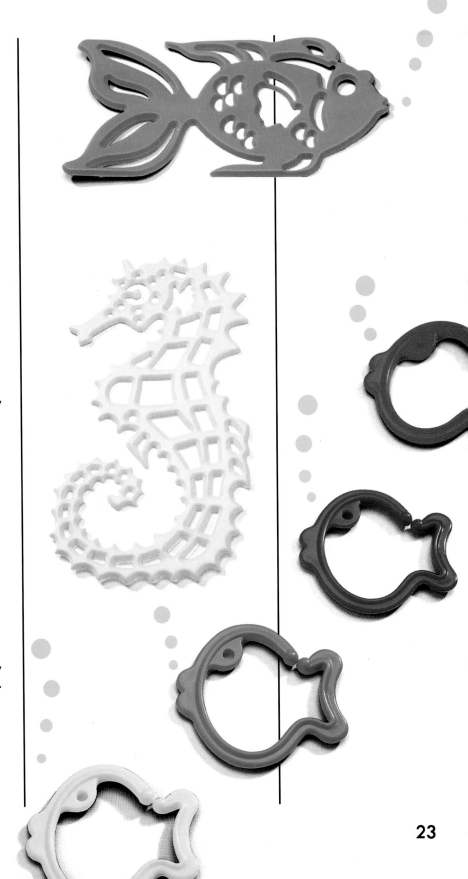

DIGGING DINOS

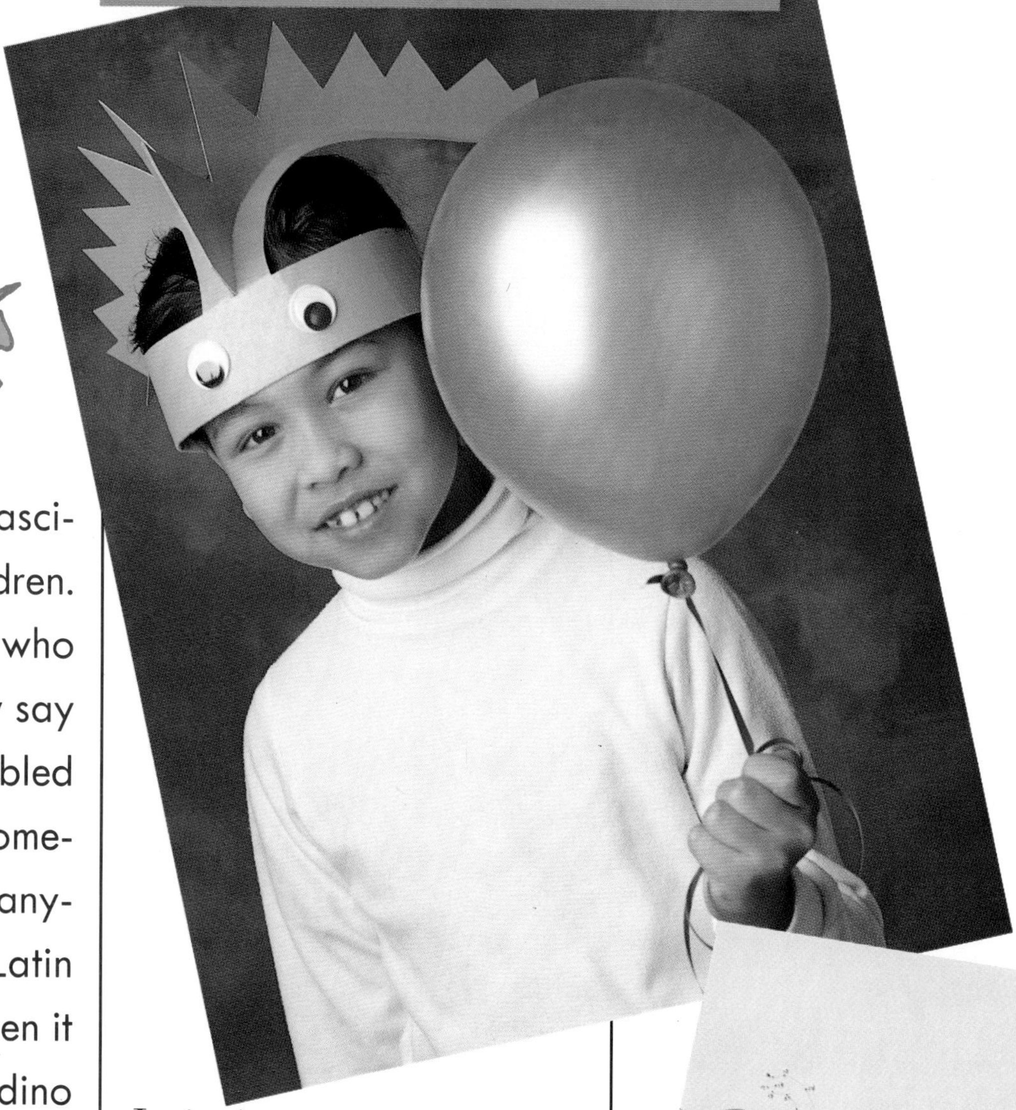

Dinosaurs fascinate children. Little ones who can barely say two-syllabled words can somehow spout many-syllabled Latin names when it comes to dino talk! This party capitalizes on the love of the beasts.

Invitation

A DOT-TO-DOT DINOSAUR lets the partygoer know what's in store when he or she pencils in the invitation. It's easy to make with a tracing from any dinosaur source.

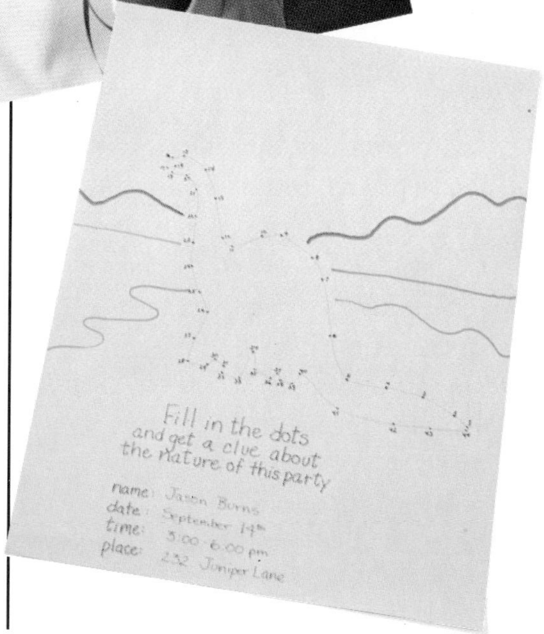

Choose a simple drawing and trace the outline of the dinosaur

Fill in the dots and get a clue about the nature of this party

name: Jason Burns
date: September 14th
time: 3:00 - 6:00 pm
place: 232 Juniper Lane

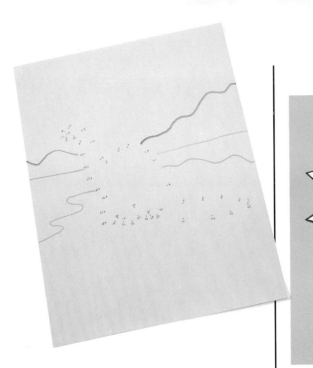

once. Mark the dot-to-dot pattern, generally keeping the dots about 1/2 inch apart. To transfer the dot design to the invitation, line up the tracing and a piece of 9 × 12-inch paper and carefully poke a pin through each dot. Remove the tracing paper, and the dot design will show up as a series of pinholes on the paper. Using a fine-tip marking pen, mark and number the dots consecutively. Add some simple scenery and your design is complete! To make multiple invitations, use a photocopier and colored paper.

Hats~Decorations

SPINY LOOKING HEAD-DRESSES transform the guests into a new breed of dino! They're easy to make and great fun to parade around in! To make the pattern, draw a 3 1/2 × 14-inch rectangle (for the band) and a 4 × 14-inch (approximately)

curved piece for the spines. Measure in about 1 1/2 inches from the front end of the spine piece and 2 inches across; make a mark and cut from the end to this point in a straight line, forming a "notch" (see photo). Draw the spine design (approximately seven spines), starting from this point. The edge opposite the spines remains unchanged.

For each headdress, trace the band once and the spine piece twice onto green poster board; cut them out. On each spine piece, carefully fold the entire curved (nonspiny) edge lengthwise, approximately 1/2 inch from the edge. Fold the band lengthwise in half. Place the two spiny pieces together, aligning the notches and the first spine. Using double-stick tape on the inside,

DIGGING DINOS

tape only the first spines together. Slide the notches inside the folded band at the center and tape it in place on the inside. Close up the band, using double-stick tape on the inside.

To complete, punch a hole near both ends of the band using a hole punch, slide a 12-inch piece of round-cord elastic through both holes, and tie closed to fit. Add two goggle eyes to the band, and you have a dino headdress!

Large DINOSAUR FOOT-PRINTS, cut from construction paper or poster board, will add to the prehistoric atmosphere. They can lead to the party site and walk along the walls!

Project

PRETZEL-DOUGH DINOS are crazy, fun, easy, and inexpensive to make. Each child is given a portion of pre-made dough to sculpt into his/her dinosaur of

choice. Popped into the oven for 15 minutes while the children enjoy the rest of the activities, the dinos are ready to go to their new homes at the party's end!

To make the dough for every four guests, measure 1½ cups of warm water and pour it into a large bowl before the party. Sprinkle in a package of yeast and stir until blended. Add a teaspoon of salt, a tablespoon of sugar, and approximately 4 cups of flour. Mix and knead the dough with your hands. Cover with plastic wrap and let it rest 2 hours.

At party time, set a table with a vinyl tablecloth or a large piece of oilcloth (available at hardware stores). Give each guest a portion of dough and a bit of flour. Encourage the guests to flour their hands and knead the dough a bit—it's half the fun! Then, they can create their own special dino! A little demonstration and a few pictures of different types of dinos might help, but this dough is pretty foolproof. The creatures should not be more than about ½ inch thick, or they'll take too long to bake. When the dinos are ready, place them on greased cookie sheets, brush them with a little bit of

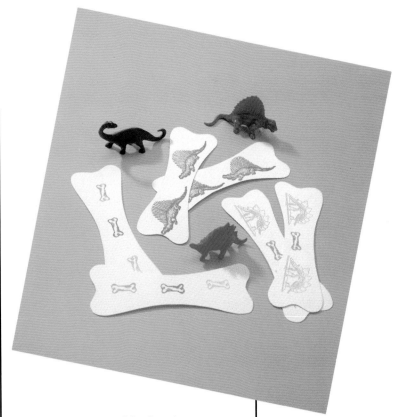

beaten egg, and bake them at 350°F for about 15 minutes. Let them cool.

Note: This project should be done early in the party to allow for cooking and cooling time.

Activities~Games

DIGGING FOR BONES—Cut out a large collection of paper bones and divide them up evenly. Color-code each group, using rubber stamps to create dino designs. Before the party, hide the bones around the party site. At party time, the children are sent scurrying to find and collect the bones. When the "dig" is over, the "MC" (Mom or a helper) calls out instructions for

DIGGING DINOS

each color or design, such as "Anyone with a red-stamped bone, tell me the name of your favorite dinosaur," or "Anyone holding two blue-stamped bones come up and roar like tyrannosaurus," etc. Be sure to call out enough instructions so that everyone feels included.

FOSSIL PRINT OBSTACLE— Roll out two long sheets of brown or white wrapping paper (or use the driveway as a surface) for the children to draw dino footprints with large pieces of chalk or crayons. Before the party, mark off squares or circles for the children to draw in, so the prints will be well-spaced apart. After the artwork is complete, it

can be used for obstacle-course relays! Divide the guests into two teams and have them speed-walk, run, hop, carry a dino "egg," roll a dino "egg," etc., around the prints!

HOOP-A-SAURUS—In this game of skill, a poster board and Contac paper brontosaurus with a hoop attached is held by the tail with one hand. The object of the game is to get the hoop on the dino's head without the help of the other hand! This is not a competitive game; it's just a lot of fun to do.

To make the hoop-a-saurus, draw a brontosaurus-like dino on paper, with a long, narrow neck and tail (for easy hoop catching and holding.) The neck

and tail should each be at least 3 inches long and the entire dino about 12 inches long. Cut out the pattern, trace onto poster board, and cut it out. Stick a piece of Contac paper on the poster-board dino and trim along the edges to fit. The addition of Contac paper gives a nice fin-ished look and it gives support to the dino for better handling.

Cut a 1¾-inch circle from a piece of poster board backed with Contac paper and trim away an inner circle to form a 1¼-inch ring. Gently lift the Contac paper away from the ring along one edge and slip in the end of a 7-inch piece of medium-weight string; press the Contac paper closed to secure the string to the ring. Tie the

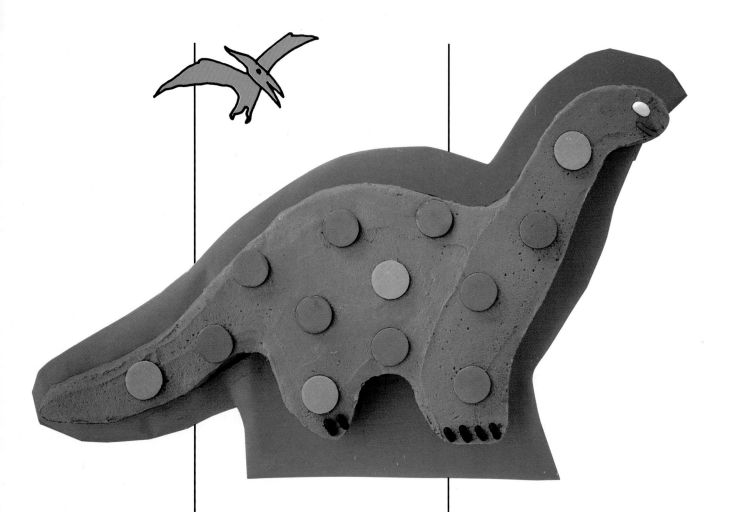

other end of the string to the dino's neck. You're ready to test your hooping abilities!

Cake~Food

DINOSAUR CAKE

CAKE & FROSTINGS
1 (13 × 9-inch) cake
2 cups Buttercream Frosting (see page 15), colored green
1 recipe Jam Glaze (see page 31)

DECORATIONS & EQUIPMENT
Assorted candies
1 (19 × 13-inch) cake board, cut to fit cake, if desired, and covered

1. Trim top and edges of cake. Using diagram 1 as a guide, draw pattern pieces on 13 × 9-inch piece of waxed paper. Cut pattern out and place on cake. Cut out dinosaur pieces.

2. Position pieces on prepared cake board as shown in diagram 2, connecting with some of the green frosting.

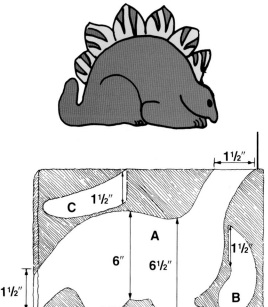

3. Brush cake lightly with Jam Glaze. Let dry about 1 hour.

4. Frost cake with green frosting.

5. Decorate with assorted candies as shown in photo.

Makes 8 to 10 servings

JAM GLAZE
   1 cup apricot or seedless rasp-
      berry jam
   1 tablespoon water

Bring jam and water to a boil in small saucepan. Remove from heat. Cool before using. Spread over cake and let stand about 1 hour before frosting.

Makes about 1 cup

Favors

The spiny dino headdress, pretzel dino, and hoop-a-saurus are wonderful mementos of this dino event. Additional possibilities are plastic figurines, stickers, and stencils, all available in numerous choices at variety and party-goods stores.

FAST TRACK

Here's your ticket onto The Fast Track a birthday party for

name _____
date _____
place _____
RSVP _____

Clip off your ticket on the line above the arrows (save!). Use the top half on your bedroom doorknob.

This high-speed event is a great choice for car enthusiasts and for a group of energy-packed guests!

Invitation

A DOORKNOB HANGER with a car and racing-flag motif delivers the party message on a clip-off admission ticket. To make it, you will need poster board; black, white, and colored Contac paper; white, rectangular stick-on labels; and 1/2-inch letters (optional). For each invitation, measure and cut a 4 × 11 1/2-inch rectangle from poster board. Cut a 2 × 3-inch keyhole to fit a doorknob, starting 3/4 inch from

the top. Draw the outline of a 1 1/2 × 1-inch racing flag and a sporty car, approximately 4 × 1 1/2 inches big; cut out the patterns. Trace the car onto colored Contac paper and flags onto white labels; cut them out. Add window and wheel details with black Contac paper and a checkerboard pattern on the two flags with permanent marking pen. For track lines, cut long,

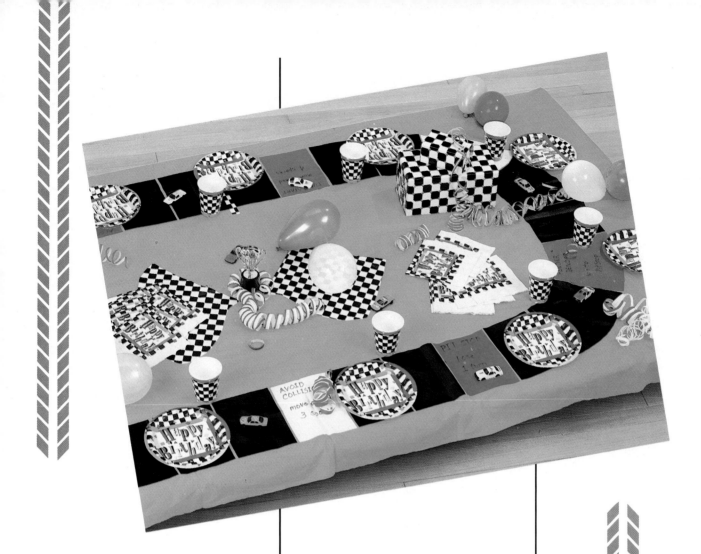

¼-inch strips of white and black Contac paper. Stick them on and trim black strips on white, placing them on the diagonal and spacing them equally apart. Write the party details on a white label(s), including a note to clip off the ticket and use the top half of the invitation as a doorknob hanger!

To assemble, stick the party label(s) on the bottom of the poster board and the track lines and car above it. Put the flags on the other side, adding black Contac paper "poles" and the words "Do Not Enter" with stick-on letters or with permanent marking pen.

Hats~Decorations

PAINTER'S CAPS with each guest's own car insignia (see project) put your guests in the driver's seat, while a RACETRACK-GAME TABLE TOPPER sets the course. It can be made from Contac paper and a green plastic tablecloth. To make it, draw half of a curved racetrack onto newspaper cut to fit half of your tabletop. Mark off the game spaces and cut them out for pat-

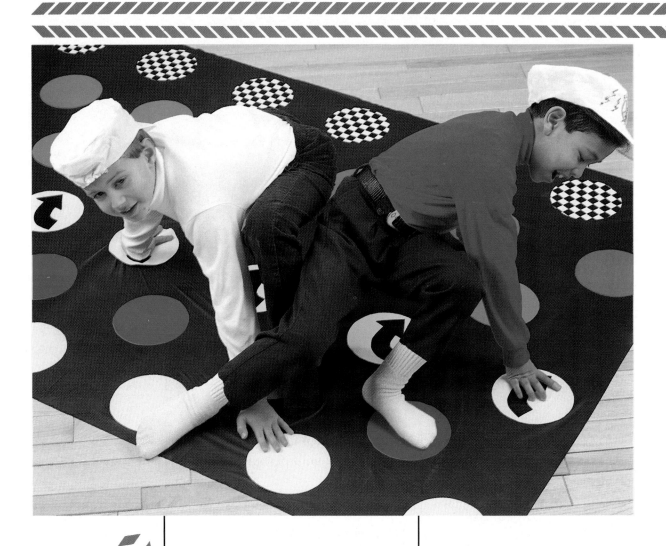

terns. Cut two of each pattern from Contac paper, using mostly black and some colors for "special" spaces. Lay out the Contac paper game spaces on the cloth to make a racetrack, mixing in colored spaces; stick the spaces onto the cloth. Add instructions on the colored spaces—"Avoid collision, move ahead three spaces," "Go to the pit stop," "Flat tire, lose a turn," etc.—

using a permanent marking pen. Playing dice and mini cars will put this game in action.

Projects

RACER CAPS are easy and fun to make, using inexpensive painter's caps, fabric and glitter pens, and paints. You can draw a car outline on the caps ahead of time and let the guests add the color and details, or you can simply give a few suggestions— a hot rod, car emblem with a lightning bolt, flaming tires, etc.—and let the kids do the rest! Give each guest a piece of cardboard to work on to keep the colors from bleeding through.

Activities~Games

GRIDLOCK—In this humorous, physical game, guests make their moves according to the throw of the dice—a right foot on a yellow light, a left hand on a turn signal! Before you know it, gridlock sets in, as hands and legs intertwine. To make this game, cut eight 7-inch circles from red, green, orange, and checkerboard Contac paper and 16 circles from yellow. Space the circles in alternating rows on a 54 × 108-inch plastic tablecloth and stick them in place. Add black "turn" arrows on eight yellow circles. Transform a pair of dice by adding a small piece of each color (including yellow with black for the turn signal) on one die, and the letters rf (right foot), lf (left foot), rh (right hand), and lh (left hand) on four sides of the other die. The remaining sides are "wild!"

To play, roll the dice and have two players move at a time. If a wild comes up, players choose what arm or leg to move. Anyone who falls or can't reach is out!

GREAT WHEEL TOSS— Transform a paper plate into a flying wheel with the addition of a checkerboard circle and cutouts (see photo). Give a "wheel" to each guest and challenge them to throw it the farthest, highest, longest, etc.!

OBSTACLE COURSE—Set up chairs, plastic garbage cans, or buckets to form two identical obstacle courses. Divide the guests into two teams and do relays around the obstacles— hopping, speed walking, egg on spoon, balloons between the legs, on all fours, and backward.

RACETRACK GAME—Using the table topper (see decorations), give each player or team a mini car as a playing piece. Roll the dice to move. First to finish wins!

MOTOR-MEMORY—Spread a collection of cars and car parts, cut from magazine pictures, on a tray. Let the guests view the tray for one minute, then take it away and ask the guests to write down what they saw. (Spelling doesn't count!)

Cake~Food

RACETRACK CAKE

CAKES & FROSTINGS
1 (9-inch) round cake
1 (13 × 9-inch) cake
1½ cups Base Frosting (see page 15), if desired
3½ cups Buttercream Frosting (see page 15)*

DECORATIONS & EQUIPMENT
Green colored sugar
2 to 3 rolls white donut-shaped hard candies, cut in half
½ (16-ounce) box cinnamon graham crackers
2- to 3-inch race cars
Flags, if desired
1 (19 × 13-inch) cake board, cut to fit cake, if desired, and covered

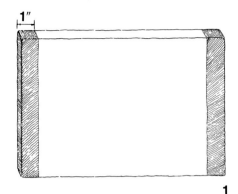

1

2

1. Trim tops and edges of cakes. Cut round cake in half crosswise. Cut 13 × 9-inch cake as shown in diagram 1.

2. Position pieces on prepared cake board as shown in diagram 2, connecting with some of the green frosting.

3. Frost entire cake with Base Frosting to seal in crumbs.

4. Using wooden pick, draw area for track, about 2 inches wide, as shown in photo. Frost center of cake with green frosting. Sprinkle with colored sugar. Frost track and sides of cake with cocoa frosting.

5. Arrange hard candies, cut-side down, around inside of track. Cut graham crackers about ¼ inch higher than cake. Arrange around edge of cake, attaching with more cocoa frosting, if needed.

6. Let frosting harden before placing cars and flags on track.

Makes 20 to 24 servings
Mix 2 cups frosting with 2 tablespoons unsweetened cocoa powder. Color remaining 1½ cups frosting green.

Favors

Racer caps and flying wheels are great take-homes. Inexpensive mini cars, car stickers, trophies, watches, winner medals, and key chains are fun prizes to add to the booty!

37

FASHION DOLL PARTY

This is a party of glamour and glitz. The fun begins as soon as the invitation arrives. The guests and their dolls are requested to come dressed for a fashion show.

Invitation

A FASHION SHOW-STYLED ANNOUNCEMENT comes tucked in a pretty little paper tote that looks like a doll-size shopping bag. To make the announcement, decorate plain stationery to create a border, using feminine stickers or a fine-tipped marking pen for a hand-drawn design. A bow or floral motif is a simple, yet fashionable choice. Write the party details

You and your doll are going to be runway models
Come dressed for the occasion
Megan's Birthday
Fashion Extravaganza!

Place: 150 BEAUTY DRIVE
Time: 1:00-4:00 PM
Date: APRIL 17TH
RSVP: 555-1414

Makeup and hairdos will be done
at the party!

within the border. Request that your guest and her doll come dressed for a fashion show. Add a note to let the guest know that she'll be getting her hair and makeup done at the party.

Slip the announcement into a paper tote. These miniature bags are available in stationery and party-supply stores. Left flat, they fit into an envelope for mailing.

Hats~Decorations

Strictly feminine is the look to aim for with pink crepe-paper streamers, cellophane and crepe-paper bows, and balloons. To make bows, cut a long length— at least 36 inches—from a roll of streamer paper and fold it in thirds. Secure the layers together in the middle with a small piece of streamer, thread, or yarn, and pull out the end pieces. For cellophane bows, fold a long piece of cellophane accordion-style, gather it together in the middle, and secure with a piece of streamer or yarn.

SET UP A HAIRDRESSING AREA—Two chairs and a small table topped with a mirror and hair and makeup supplies will do. Fill a trunk with scarves, inexpensive feather boas, hats, gloves, and frilly fabric pieces.

Projects

Making glamorous jewelry is great fun for everyone, particularly when it is easy and fun. The materials required for clay jewelry are few. Low-temperature, fast-baking, nontoxic clays are widely available in craft and toy stores. The colors are fabulous. Adding white to strong colors and blending them will turn the basic clays into a color wheel to work with. Kids (and adults) will enjoy making marbled beads (twisted strings of clay rolled into a bead), medallions, and little sculptures that can be used on earrings, necklaces, bracelets, hair beads, and pins. Put wide pinholes or stick U-shaped wire pieces into the clay jewelry items and they are ready to bake!

A designated baker, an adult or older baby-sitter, helps move the project along. Before baking, check to make sure the holes for string and other findings are big

FASHION DOLL PARTY

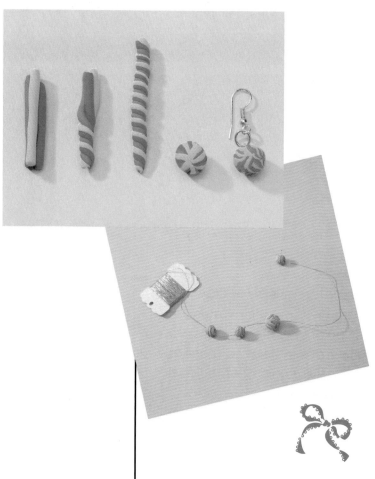

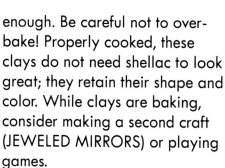

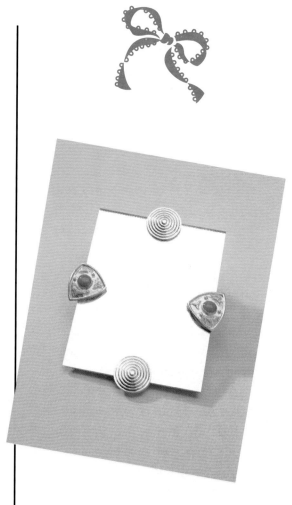

enough. Be careful not to over-bake! Properly cooked, these clays do not need shellac to look great; they retain their shape and color. While clays are baking, consider making a second craft (JEWELED MIRRORS) or playing games.

To assemble the jewelry, elastic gold thread, round-cord elastic, pin bases, earring hooks and clip-ons, and ring jumpers are all that is required for most projects. Stringing can be done by the

girls. You may need a jumper ring to attach a flat piece to a fish hook earring and white glue to attach pieces to clip-on earrings. An adult should do these finishing steps.

JEWELED MIRRORS are a fast, exciting project. Plain 4 × 6-inch mirrors, with a picture hanger added on the back before the party, can be decorated with cheap clip-on earrings. Just clip the earrings along the edges.

Breakable mirrors should be handled gently and bits of felt can be added to protect the mirror. If your mirror has very sharp edges, be sure to tape the edges. Have fun buying clip-ons in the sale bins!

Activities~Games

GETTING A SPECIAL HAIR-DO—Invite an older sister, neighbor, or professional hairdresser to help out as a hairstylist. Guests can take turns getting a glamour "do" for the fashion show. French braids, beehives, and ponytails are fun to wear and easy to create. For health reasons, you may want to tell each girl to bring her own labeled brush.

A MAKEOVER—A little eye shadow, blush, and lipstick go a long way with little girls. Your stylist may handle this or you may have another person act as a beauty consultant. Again, for health reasons, use new makeup and apply it with disposable cotton swabs.

PUTTING ON A FASHION SHOW—When everyone is beautified, the girls with their dolls should take turns parading down a "runway," while you or another adult MCs the show. Have fun and be silly as you point out some of the outstanding features of the child and her doll's costume. Let the guests rummage through the trunk for last-minute, finishing touches and remember to play soft, swinging music in the background!

An instant snapshot of each girl as she walks down the runway would be great!

Cake~Food

For something simple, quick, and fun, decorate a traditional cake with flowers, pink bows, and the sentiment, "Happy Birthday, Beautiful!"

Favors

The girls will take home the jewelry and mirrors they made and their snapshot. Other ideas are fun beads and earrings, bubble bath, perfume, inexpensive feather boas, a fashion-doll coloring book, or paper-doll set.

ROYAL BALL

The charisma of royalty is irresistible to most children. So many of their fictional friends are of royal descent that many children secretly believe they are royal, too!

Invitation

A ROYAL DECREE attached to a PRINCESS PAPER DOLL will send the invitee straight to fantasy heaven. THE ROYAL DECREE is written on plain paper, in your best fancy printing. The wording

The House of Miller cordially invites you to attend A Royal Ball honoring the lovely Emily on the twelfth of October 2:00~4:00pm 12 Castle Lane Drive RSVP 555~1313

Please decorate the Princess Paper Doll and bring her to the Ball!

of the invitation should have a royal flair. (The Royal Family, or the House of Smith, requests the honor of your presence at a ball honoring the birthday of Princess Chelsea (your child's name). The date is written out as the 14th day of the 4th month in the year one thousand, nine hundred, etc. Instructions to decorate the paper doll enclosed should be added at the end of the invitation, with a reminder to bring the finished, dressed princess along to the party. The more princesses, the merrier. Gold-foil seals, available at stationery stores, are the perfect closure for this royal invitation. ◆

PRINCESS PAPER DOLLS can be homemade or store bought. To make your own, draw or trace a simple outline of a princess figure on paper. Transfer the drawing onto the flat side of white poster board. Go over the outlines with a narrow black marker. Cut the figure out, leaving the black lines. Enthusiastic hostesses may want to include tidbits (lace, fun fur, beads, glitter, sequins, tiny faux pearls, swatches of velvet or ultra suede, etc.) in a plastic bag for the kids to use in decorating their princesses.

Hats~Decorations

CROWNS can be purchased at party-supply stores or be homemade, using poster board. Add jewels (stick-on earrings, pieces of metallic papers, glitter,

sequins, beads, or craft jewels) and personalize the crowns by adding the guest's name in glitter for a custom look befitting a princess.

THRONES are a dramatic addition to the storybook quality of this party. A simple coat of arms decoration for the dining table chairs can be made from felt or poster board. With the addition of helium balloons tied at each side of the chair and the coat of arms, chairs will take on the appearance of a throne. To make the COAT OF ARMS, first make a pattern on newspaper to fit your chairs. Finish the pattern by folding the paper in half vertically and trimming to ensure symmetry. (The width of the coat of arms shown in the photo is

nearly equal to the length, the curve beginning at three-fifths the length.) Pin the pattern to the felt, cut out felt shields for a base, and decorate with simple different-colored felt cut-outs (castles, crowns, etc.), strung sequins, glitter, ribbons, and braid. Add ribbon ties or felt tabs to the top outer edges to attach the shield to the chair. All of these can be added with white glue. If your chairs have solid backs with no place onto which to tie the coat of arms, make a second shield, attach it at the top to the decorated shield with either white glue, ribbon ties, or felt tabs, and drape it over the front and back of the chair. For simplicity's sake, make all the shields with the same design.

The BANQUET TABLE should be coordinated with the shields if you choose to make them. A coordinating cloth or a gold tablecloth will complete the look. Each guest's decorated princess paper doll should be displayed in the center of the table.

Projects

There are many fabulous projects with a royal theme. Children adore decorating crowns and simple store-bought masks to

wear to a ball. Making SUGAR CUBE CASTLES seems to be a favorite. The materials required for this project are sugar cubes (more than ½ box per child), icing for mortar (see recipe on page 45), small candies (gumdrops, candy-coated chocolates, shoestring licorice), and a sturdy foil-covered cardboard base (7- or 8-inch square made in advance of the party). Each child is given a mound of icing and a craft stick or plastic knife. The mortar is either spread on or put on by dipping the cubes in icing. Remind the children that the foundation (first layer of sugar cubes) must be stuck to the base with icing. Wide rather than tall castles are the sturdiest. Make a sample in advance to explore

technique, and set it center stage to inspire the children.

Activities~Games

THE ROYAL TREASURE HUNT, a theme scavenger hunt, sends the kids looking around for one of each type of hidden royal treasure. A JEWEL BAG, made from fun fur or velvet-type fabric (two seams and a drawstring), large enough to hold the loot, adds to the excitement. Treasures can include gold-foil wrapped chocolate coins, polished stone rings, foreign stamps, pictures clipped from magazines featuring real royalty, face cards of playing cards, wax seals printed on small pieces of paper, and other regal items. Make sure to hide plenty of each item for each child so that no one feels left out and everyone gets a few prizes.

THE ROYAL CHALLENGE is a mental game in which groups or individuals must name royalty when given clues such as "Who lost her shoe?" or "She was a princess under the sea and a queen on land."

THE ROYAL GAMES are a group of active games reminiscent of jousting matches. These contests of skill should be played as team relays. Giving each team royal family names like Montague or Capulet will make it all seem exotic. Suggestions for relays include: racing with a coin balanced on the back of your hand; stepping through a hula-hoop and passing it over your head to the next child; keeping a balloon in the air as you run the length of the course; or dressing in a costume, undressing, and passing the costume along to the next teammate.

Icing

Beat two egg whites until stiff. Gradually add 3 cups sifted confectioners' sugar until the icing is of thick spreading consistency. Add red food coloring until desired pink color is achieved.

ROYAL BALL

Cake~Food

CASTLE CAKE

CAKES & FROSTINGS
  3 (8-inch) square cakes
  2 cups Base Frosting (see page 15), if desired
  5¼ cups Buttercream Frosting (see page 15)*

DECORATIONS & EQUIPMENT
  Assorted colored sugar
  4 sugar ice cream cones
  Small purple and white gumdrops
  Pastel candy-coated chocolate pieces
  2 pink sugar wafer cookies
  1 (19 × 13-inch) cake board, cut in half crosswise and covered

1. Trim tops and edges of cakes. Place one square cake on prepared cake board. Frost top with some of the white frosting.

2. Cut remaining cakes as shown in diagrams 1 and 2.

3. Place piece A over bottom layer. Frost top of piece A with some of the white frosting.

4. Position remaining pieces as shown in diagram 3, connecting with some of the white frosting.

5. Frost entire cake with Base Frosting to seal in crumbs.

6. Frost again with white frosting. Cover piece D (bridge) with colored sugar.

7. Frost cones with blue and yellow frostings. Place as shown in photo.

8. Decorate castle and towers as shown, using frosting to attach candies, if needed.

9. Arrange wafer cookies on front of castle for gate.

Makes 24 to 28 servings

Tip: For easier frosting of cones, hold cone over fingers of one hand while frosting with the other hand. Place in position, touching up frosting, if needed.

*Color ½ cup frosting blue and ½ cup yellow; reserve 4¼ cups white frosting.

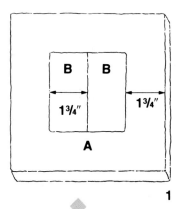

B   B

$1^3/_4''$ $1^3/_4''$

A

1

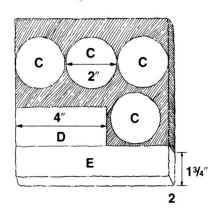

C   C
2''

C   C

4''
D

E $1^3/_4''$

2

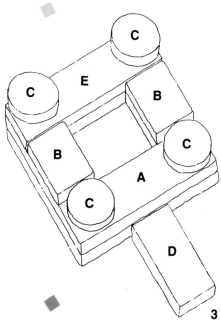

C

C   E   B

B   C

A

C

D

3

Entertainment

Classical music playing in the background creates a great atmosphere. A family friend or local teenager can dress up like a court jester and perform tricks (juggling, card tricks), or tell jokes as they help with the kids. A baby-sitter dressed up like a "real" princess or friendly dragon, or a fairy tale puppet show (professional or amateur) are other alternatives.

Favors

The guests will take home their project, the throne coat of arms, paper doll, crowns, and all the loot in their jewel bags. Other ideas for regal favors include storybooks, fairy tale coloring books or paper dolls, an inexpensive "glass slipper" or crown (available at bridal, craft, or toy stores), a fairy princess wand, and castle figurines.

FRIGHT NIGHT

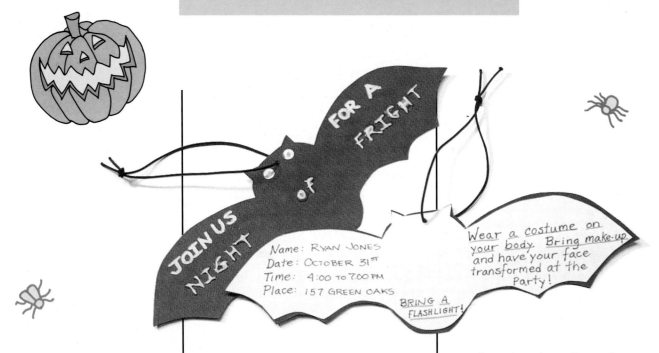

Name: RYAN JONES
Date: OCTOBER 31ST
Time: 4:00 TO 7:00 PM
Place: 157 GREEN OAKS

JOIN US FOR A NIGHT OF FRIGHT

BRING A FLASHLIGHT!

Wear a costume on your body. Bring make-up and have your face transformed at the party!

Capitalizing on the darker elements of the night makes this party an event to remember at Halloween or anytime when a little spooking is in order!

Invitation

A black paper bat delivers the glow-in-the-dark message, beckoning the guest to come to a NIGHT OF FRIGHT. Along with the party details written on the back, all guests are asked to come dressed in costume on their bodies only (the frightful faces will be added at the party) and to bring along some face make-up and a flashlight labeled with their name. To make the invitation, draw a simple bat shape, sized to fit into a standard envelope. Trace and cut bats from black poster board and white paper. Glue a white bat onto a black bat. Fill in the party details on the white bat. Print the message, "Join Us for a Night of Fright" on the black side, using a fluorescent marker for the first four words and glow-in-the-dark paint for the words "Night of Fright." Glow-in-the-dark paint is available at craft stores and at Halloween headquarters. It paints on easily and glows in the dark without special lighting. Add two eyes and a piece of black thread or round-cord elastic for hanging the bat.

Hats~Decorations

A SPIDERWEB GAME, created out of yarn, and black, fuzzy spiders are visual reminders of the spook factor of this party, as

well as part of a great activity. Hanging bats that glow in the dark add to the atmosphere!

The game takes up a whole room or more and must be set up before the party. As a result, the activity connected with it should be planned for the beginning of the gathering, or the web should be set up in an area that does not interfere with the other party plans. To create the web, attach one end of a ball of different colored yarn to a piece of cardboard for each guest. Unwind each ball, running the string in and around the objects in the room(s)—over chairs, around doorways, under tables, etc.—weaving the yarn as you do to create a huge web effect! At the yarn ends—which should be located in different, hidden places—attach a big, fuzzy spider or a treat. CREEPY LOOKING SPIDERS are easy to make with 2-inch black pompons and

black chenille pipe cleaners. Simply wrap and twist four pipe cleaners around a pompon and bend to shape the legs. To create GLOWING FLYING BATS, draw and cut large bats from black poster board. Paint the edges with glow-in-the-dark paint (if desired). Make two small holes about 1/2 inch apart in the center of each bat and weave through, knotting a long piece of black round-cord elastic. Hang from the ceiling or doorways. At some point during the party when the children are seated, turn the lights off to get the glowing effect of the bats!

Projects

GHOUL HANDS—Pieces of black or colored poster board,

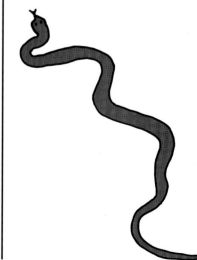

cut in simple, knobby hand shapes, are transformed into ghoul hands with the addition of colored and glitter glue, glow-in-the-dark paint, round stickers, sequins, goggle eyes, crazy paper shapes, etc. Give each child a pair of hands with a piece of round-cord elastic slipped through two small holes near the wrists and tied. The elastic holds the finished hands on the wearer!

GETTING GHOULISH—Using the makeup the guests have brought, plus a few other specialties—professional blackout for blackened teeth or face putty for warts—an adult and/or a teen helper makes up the children's faces to go with their costumes and ghoul hands.

Activities~Games

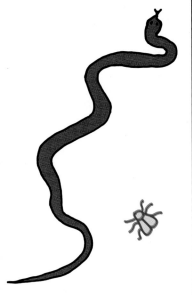

SPOOK BOX—For younger children, a decorated refrigerator box or large wardrobe box can be used for picture taking. Wrap three sides of the box in black crepe or tissue paper. Add a purchased or homemade picture of a witch, pumpkin, ghost, etc., with a mouth opening large enough for a head to peek through, onto each of the three covered sides. Cut the corre-sponding mouth opening in the box. Cut an opening in the fourth side for the children to step into the box. At party time, let children choose which scary thing they want to be and have them peek their head through the thing's mouth for a picture.

WORD SCRAMBLE—Each guest is given a list of words relating to the night—nocturnal animal names, horror shows, night shows, scary characters—written in scrambled form on a bat. Their task is to unscramble them.

SPOOK SPIN—A spinner is made from poster board and a brass clasp for a game of dare for all ages. Cut out a large circle of poster board and a spinner-shaped piece. Divide the circle up evenly into 16 segments,

using a ruler and pencil. Write a dare in each segment, such as "Pretend to be a vampire," "Howl like a coyote," "Make five scary faces," etc. Punch a hole through the center and add the spinner and clasp; make sure the spinner moves freely.

Cake~Food

SPIDERWEB CAKE

CAKE & FROSTINGS
   1 (9-inch) round cake
   1 cup Base Frosting (see page 15), if desired
   2 cups Buttercream Frosting (see page 15)*

DECORATIONS & EQUIPMENT
   2 black licorice candies or jelly beans
   1 black licorice whip
   1 (10-inch) round cake board, covered, or large plate
   Pastry bag and medium writing tip

1. Trim top of cake. Place on prepared cake board.

2. Frost entire cake with Base Frosting to seal in crumbs.

3. Frost again with blue frosting.

4. Using writing tip and white frosting, pipe 4 concentric circles, about 1 inch apart, and a dot in the center of the cake.

5. Using spatula or tip of knife, draw through circles at regular intervals, as shown in photo above, alternating direction each time.

6. Place candies for spider's body and head on cake. Cut 8 licorice whip pieces; curve and arrange for legs.

Makes 10 to 12 servings

Color 1½ cups frosting blue; reserve ½ cup white frosting.

Variation: Can also be made as a 2-layer cake. Use two 9-inch round cakes and increase blue frosting to 2½ cups; decorate as above.

Favors

Ghoul hands, spiders, piñata fillings, and chocolate spiders are great take-homes. Paperback mystery books wrapped with black ribbon (for older kids), glow-in-the-dark wands or lite sticks, fake tattoos, and other creepy things are great purchasable options.

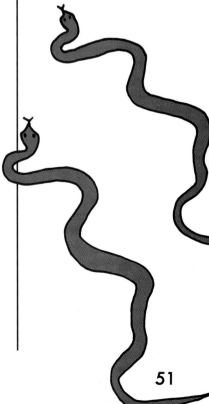

CREATURES FROM OUTER SPACE

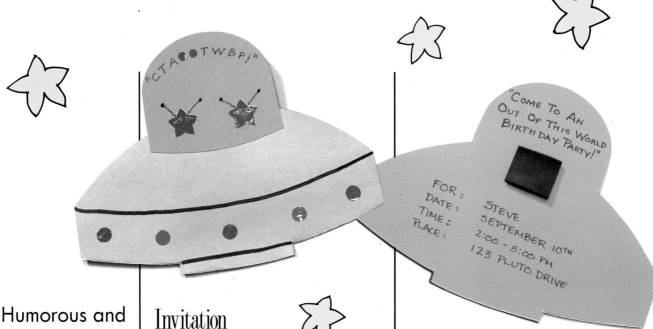

Humorous and monsterlike, this party allows children to use their imaginations to create a creature from outer space and to pretend to be aliens themselves!

Invitation

A MAGNETIZED FLYING SAUCER delivers the party message in an alien tongue via an alphabet-coded message, "C.T.A.O.O.T.W.B.P!" The translation appears on back, "Come to an out-of-this world birthday party!" To make the invitation, draw a flying saucer—to fit into an envelope—using the invitation in the photo as a guide; cut out along the outline. Trace the pattern onto silver-faced poster board or onto poster board that has been covered on one side with silver Contac paper; cut out along the outline. Trace the

upper rounded edge of the invitation onto brightly colored paper and join it to the silver piece with a straight line to form the "cockpit." Cut it out. Stick the "cockpit" onto the invitation with double-stick tape. Print the alien code across the top and add two stick-on circles or stars for aliens. To complete the look, stick on eyes and add antennae with a marking pen. Turn the invitation over and spell out the coded message, writing the first letter of each word in a different color. Add the party details and a small piece of magnetic tape.

Hats~Decorations

Turning the party scene into an invasion of aliens is easy with crazy-looking poster-board ALIEN BANDS. Make a pattern, starting with a $1\frac{1}{2} \times 14$-inch rectangular band. Add two squiggly lined projectiles, approximately 7 inches tall, along one long edge, positioning each slightly off-center. If desired, draw two smaller projectiles in part of the remaining space. Draw another, same-sized band and add two projectiles, slightly off-center to the projectiles on the first band; cut both patterns out. Trace patterns onto two different colors of poster board; cut them out (see photo). Align both bands together and bend the projectiles from the first band over onto the second band; double-stick tape in place. Add cat's eyes or goggle eyes where desired to complete the look. Punch holes near the ends of the band and tie closed to fit around the head with a piece of round-cord elastic.

Projects

PICTURE AN ALIEN—Give the kids a chance to create their idea of an alien, using an assortment of crazy notions. When complete, each guest gets a chance to picture him/herself in the alien's shoes by putting his/her face in the "peek through."

A large piece of foam core, available at art-supply stores, is a good base for this project. Draw and cut out the face opening close to the top of the foam core. Using a colored marker, draw in a curvy lined alien body shape. At party time, have an assortment of stickers, pompons, goggle eyes, colored foam, feathers, sequins, netting, streamer paper, crayons or washable

CREATURES FROM OUTER SPACE

ALIEN HANDS—Have the kids create their own set of alien hands. See instructions for GHOUL HANDS in the Fright Night chapter.

Activities~Games

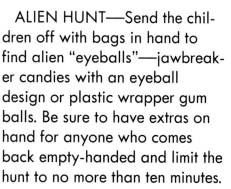

ALIEN HUNT—Send the children off with bags in hand to find alien "eyeballs"—jawbreaker candies with an eyeball design or plastic wrapper gum balls. Be sure to have extras on hand for anyone who comes back empty-handed and limit the hunt to no more than ten minutes.

ALIEN PHOTO—Take an instant photo of each child sticking his or her head through the opening of the picture-an-alien backdrop.

PERSON, PERSON, ALIEN—While the photos are being taken, amuse the children who are waiting with an alien version of "Duck, Duck, Goose." Arrange them in a circle and have someone be "IT." IT goes around the circle, tapping each child on the head, while saying "Person." After a number of "Person" calls, IT says "Alien!," and the child

markers, and/or whatever colorful odds and ends you can find or have readily available. Have double-stick tape, paste, or glue available for sticking the notions on. The addition of a few holes on the body is helpful for securing some decorations in place, as are large round stick-on circles or squares (the less drippy glue, the better). Start this project early in the party to allow for drying, picture-taking, and a game of toss later on.

tapped with this word must get up, run after IT, and try to catch IT before IT takes the Alien's place in the circle. If IT gets to the Alien's place before being tagged, the Alien becomes "IT."

ALIEN PIÑATA—Papier-mâché a large round balloon with a strong rubber band or light rope attached; let dry and spray-paint it silver. Add a few paper spirals with eyes for decoration (if desired), cut a small opening near the top, and you have a piñata ready to fill with candies. Note: Be sure you have enough room and plenty of supervision for this game. Use a plastic bat or similar object for hitting the piñata. Have extra candies on hand for children who don't collect many.

ALIEN ADVENTURES—Create or copy a series of short "out-of-

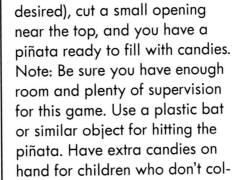

FEED THE ALIEN—Use the picture-an-alien backdrop for a game of toss. Kids try to throw rolled-up tissue balls or foam-rubber balls through the face opening.

Cake~Food

ALIEN CAKE

CAKES & FROSTINGS
  1 (9-inch) round cake
  1 (8-inch) square cake
  1 cup Base Frosting (see page 15), if desired
  3½ cups Buttercream Frosting (see page 15)*

DECORATIONS & EQUIPMENT
  Assorted candies or gumballs
  Pink and white sugar wafer cookies
  1 (19 × 13-inch) cake board, cut in half crosswise and covered
  Pastry bags and basketweave tip

1. Trim tops and edges of cakes. Cut round cake as shown in diagram 1.

2. Position pieces on prepared cake board as shown in diagram 2, connecting with some of the blue frosting. Trim sides of round cake to match sides of square cake, if necessary.

3. Frost entire cake with Base Frosting to seal in crumbs.

4. Using wooden pick, draw line across cake 1 inch up from bottom.

this-world" stories and replace a number of the words with a series of blanks. Have kids call out requested words—a noun, verb, adjective, funny-sounding word, etc.—to fill in the blanks, and then read the new version of the story. This is a humorous, calming game for the kids!

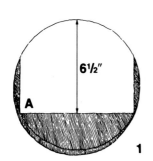

6½"

A

1

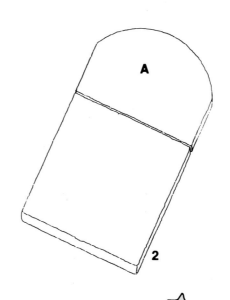

A

2

Frost area with some of the white frosting as shown in photo. Frost remaining square cake with some of the blue frosting.

5. Draw line 4 inches above frosted blue area. Frost area with gray frosting.

6. Divide remaining area in half vertically; frost areas in blue and white frosting as shown, reserving small portion of each color for piping.

7. Using flat side of basketweave tip and reserved white frosting, pipe vertical line dividing white and blue frosting.

8. Using flat side of basketweave tip and reserved blue frosting, pipe border between blue and gray frosting as shown.

9. Decorate with assorted candies and wafer cookies as shown.

Makes 16 to 20 servings

Color 1½ cups frosting blue and 1 cup gray; reserve 1 cup white frosting.

Favors

The alien headbands, hands, snapshot, and hunt and piñata goodies are great take-home favors. Store-bought possibilities could include anything slimy or ugly looking, such as green slime or candy worms.

CAROLING PARTY

Put a little fa-la-la-la-la into your holidays by hosting a children's caroling party.

Invitation

To make a MUSICAL INVITA-TION, photocopy sheet music (preferably a Christmas carol) on white, green, or red paper. Trim and fold in half, making a card that will fit into a standard envelope. Add a strip of metallic tape (available at craft and hardware stores) to the outside top and bottom of the card. Include a request for children to bring a grab-bag gift no larger than 3 inches, costing under $1.

Hats~Decorations

Since your home is already dressed for the holidays, addi-tional decorations are not required. You might consider having the guests trim a small children's tree in the party room while waiting for everyone to arrive. Purchasing ornaments is not necessary. Cookie cutters, paper cutouts, tissue paper bows, ribbons, cookies, and other items lying around the house make wonderful tree decorations. Tie the ornaments to the tree with ribbon, yarn, or pipe cleaners for a special touch.

Projects

Beautiful, sturdy little COOKIE HOUSES can be made using purchased butter cookies, icing (see page 59), foil-covered card-board, and holiday candies. Have whole cookies on hand for

the foundations, roofs, and the long sides of the houses. Cut two square house end pieces from whole cookies for every house you plan to make at the party. Just before the party begins, make the icing. Cover the bowl with a damp cloth to keep the icing from becoming hard. To construct the houses, children apply icing wherever the cookies meet, and on the sides and roof to attach candies.

Have children put the finishing touches on their own HOLIDAY CALENDARS. The materials for this project include white poster board or heavy drawing paper, a craft knife, a second colored paper, and small or tiny stickers for inside the windows. Choose a shape for the calendar. Cut a calendar front from white poster board and matching backing from colored paper. Determine the number of windows you will need for the calendar and their size. Cut along three sides of

each window with a craft knife on the calendar front piece. Match the calendar front to its backing and trace the window placement onto the backing. Have the calendars finished to this point before the party. Using art materials you provide (glitter pens, markers, sequins, and stickers), children decorate the front and inside of their holiday calendars. (Remind the children not to stick their windows closed!) Carefully match the front to the backing and staple together along the edges for a finished project.

Icing

Beat two egg whites until stiff. Gradually add 3 cups sifted confectioners' sugar until the icing is of thick spreading consistency.

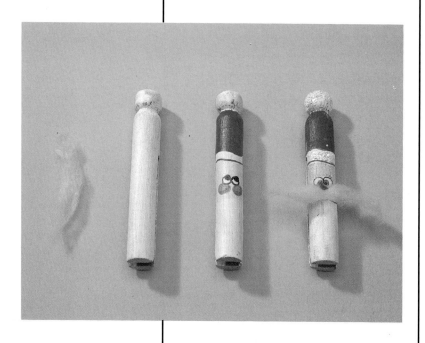

songs. A simple cover illustration, a bell tied to the book with a ribbon, or fancy lettering make the book of carols an item your guests will want to keep. Sing Christmas carols to instrumental accompaniment, to the tunes on a holiday tape or CD, or a cappella.

After the guests arrive, take their grab-bag gifts into another room and wrap them into surprise balls/snowballs using rolls of white crepe-paper streamers. Pass the SURPRISE SNOWBALLS around the circle of guests toward the end of the party.

A game of DONUT CHOMP will liven the mood of any group. To set up this game, hang donuts on strings or ribbons from a clothesline. The donuts should be hanging at the children's face level. The challenge for party-goers is to eat their own donut off the ribbon with no hands!

MITTEN PAIRS, a competitive scored hunt, involves the children searching out hidden pairs of mittens and gloves. The game rule is that once you pick up a glove or mitten you cannot pick up another unless it is the match to the one you are holding. Don't forget to check out the other guests' selection!

CLOTHESPIN ORNAMENTS are a quick party project. Paint clothespins white with acrylic or poster paint before the party. Children transform the clothespins into Santas with basic art supplies (markers, white glitter, cotton balls, red felt dots for noses, and glue). The knob on the clothespin becomes the top of Santa's hat, and the side of the clothespin his face.

Activities~Games

Since CAROLING is the centerpiece of the party, make an effort to provide a book containing the words of popular Christmas

Cake~Food

Seasonal cookies, drinks (hot cider, hot chocolate, holiday punch), and popcorn balls are great snack foods to serve at this party.

POPCORN BALLS

2½ quarts popped popcorn
½ cup corn syrup
⅓ cup water
1 cup sugar
½ teaspoon salt
¼ cup butter or margarine, cut into pieces
1 teaspoon vanilla
Food coloring

EQUIPMENT
Candy Thermometer

1. Pour popcorn into large heat-proof bowl; set aside.

2. Combine corn syrup, water, sugar, and salt in medium saucepan. Cook over medium heat, stirring constantly, until sugar dissolves and mixture comes to a boil. Wash down side of pan with pastry brush frequently dipped in hot water to remove sugar crystals.

3. Add candy thermometer. Continue to cook until mixture reaches the hard-ball stage (255°F). Remove from heat.

4. Whisk in butter and vanilla. Add food coloring, a few drops at a time, until desired color is obtained. Immediately pour sugar mixture over popcorn, stirring until completely coated. Spread popcorn on 2 large baking sheets.

5. Cool slightly and shape in balls or leave as clusters.

Makes about 3 quarts

HINT: Remove any unpopped kernels before measuring the popped popcorn.

Favors

The Christmas carol book, craft project, and grab-bag gift are holiday treasures for every guest. Other favor suggestions include a tape of Christmas carols, cool socks, mittens, hats, and other theme products.

PARTY SHORTS

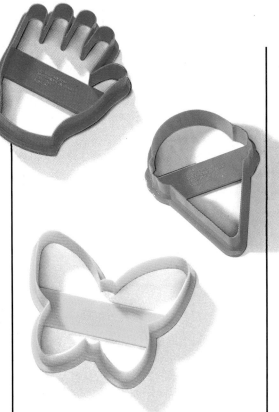

Here are a few other party ideas to tickle your imagination. They're called "party shorts" because they don't go into a lot of detail, but are certainly fun options to think about!

COOKING PARTY

Kids love to cook, especially in the company of friends. Tuck an invitation in the pocket of an envelope-sized paper apron to announce the event. Make an oilcloth chef's apron for each guest and have the children design their own pizzas and dessert—chocolate-covered fruit and pretzels! A homemade cookbook featuring kids' recipes for slime, pretzel dough, jewelry clay, milkshakes, pizza, etc., is a real party-favor hit.

BICYCLE PARADE

Develop a party around decorating bicycles and ride toys. Provide festive-looking decorating materials—colorful crepe-paper streamers, feathers, fuzzy pipe cleaners, flowers, playing cards or poster-board pieces, and spring-mounted clothespins for holding the cards on the wheel spokes—and have the kids make their own "vanity" license plates! Consider bicycle accessories—baskets, horns, or bells—for favors. End the party with a parade.

NATURE PARTY

Combine a nature walk with a birthday party for a real nature-lover's treat! Just make fun-fur raccoon hats for the children and get them involved in decorating trees and vegetation. The rest of the time can be spent rock-painting, doing animal calls, and playing animal-theme games.

TEA PARTY

The fun only begins when "ladies are invited to tea" with purse-shaped invitations. Continue the theme with decorated straw hats, pretty picture frames, dress-up games, and, of course, an official tea. Add to the fun with Mom and another helper serving the girls in starched aprons and dark dresses. Refreshment ideas include petit-fours, cupcakes, cookies, heart-shaped sandwiches, and lemonade or iced tea.

DINNER PARTY

Put the kids in your shoes. Throw a formal dinner party from hors d'oeuvres to dessert, served by adults in uniform! Beautifully written invitations for this evening event request the guests to come dressed in their Sunday best. Dim the lights, put on background music, and break out the silver!

COME-AS-YOU-ARE

Telephone invitations yield a surprising result. Guests are requested to come to the party wearing what they had on when they were called and invited. Calling at odd hours will ensure a humorous mixture of dress!

SPORTING EVENTS

Personalize your birthday party trip to a sporting event. Equip each car with a visual scavenger hunt list for an en-route competition. Play auto "baseball," advancing players through the bases when sports trivia questions are correctly answered. Send the kids off with personalized water bottles, ball caps, stocking caps, or other sporting accessories.

HAPPY TRAILS

An old-West theme party is always a classic. Simple "WANTED" poster invitations can quickly get everyone in the right mood. Request the guests to come in blue jeans so that they will fit right into your house— now transformed into a Western town with posters, signs, and other decorations. Make all of the guests felt "Sheriff" vests and badges so they square-dance and participate in the fun.

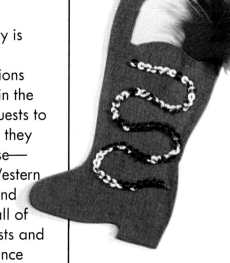

63

PARTY SHORTS

PUTTING ON THE LIPS

A lip-synching celebration may be just the thing to bring out the shier guests. A backdrop for performances can be easily constructed from a black plastic tablecloth and neon-colored cutouts of musical notes, stars, lips, and lightning bolts. To break the ice, a simple lip-synching game to popular tunes can begin the fun while someone videotapes the event for future viewing. Funky costumes can make the game all the more appealing.

FLYING PARTY

Paper airplanes really get this party off the ground. Kids create their own special airplanes, using designs and decorations. Flight competitions are the perfect follow-up. Check out your local library or bookstore for paper-airplane design books.

POOL PARTY

Capitalizing on the fact that guests are in bathing suits is a great time to play water-balloon games—basketball, volleyball, tossing relays, etc.

GIRL-TALK SLEEP-OVER

Get the most out of a sleep-over without losing too much sleep! Guests create a run-on diary entry in which each takes a turn "writing" the continuing saga of the birthday girl. "Telephone" and games of social daring ("sing the Star-Spangled Banner while standing on your head," etc.) add to the girl talk. Making sachets and having a midnight snack cap off the evening.

AZTEC ADVENTURE

Boys will just love to "make-believe" they are part of a dangerous adventure. Help them in their game with coded invitations, papier-mâché snakes, obstacle-course games, and hidden treasures.